MW01222793

ANTS

Written by Graham Meadows & Claire Vial

CONTENTS

About Ants 2

What Ants Look Like 4

Their Nests 6

The Members of an Ant Colony 10

How Ants Collect Food 12

   Scavengers 14

   Hunters 15

   Harvesters 17

   Gardeners 17

   Honeydew Collectors 18

Their Life Cycle 20

Ants and Their Importance to Humans 22

   How They Are Useful 22

   How They Are Harmful 23

Glossary .24

Index 24

Dominie Press, Inc.

ABOUT ANTS

Ants belong to the same group of insects as wasps and bees. Scientists have discovered about 9,000 **species** of ants, but there could be many more. They are one of the most common insects on Earth.

Although ants can be found almost everywhere in the world, they are most common in **tropical** and subtropical areas. They are not found in the Arctic or Antarctic.

Ants live in a variety of **habitats**, including deserts, rainforests, mountains, and swamps.

Many people think that termites are a type of ant because they are sometimes called "white ants." However, the two insects are not related.

▲ **Bulldog Ant**

▲ **White-footed House Ants in a Nest**

WHAT ANTS LOOK LIKE

The ant's body is divided into three parts: the head, the thorax, and the abdomen. It has three pairs of legs and a pair of **antennae**. The antennae are used for smelling, touching, tasting, and hearing.

◀ **Leafcutter Ant**

Ants use their strong jaws to carry objects such as food, and for chewing and digging.

Most ants are black or brown. A few species are brightly colored.

4

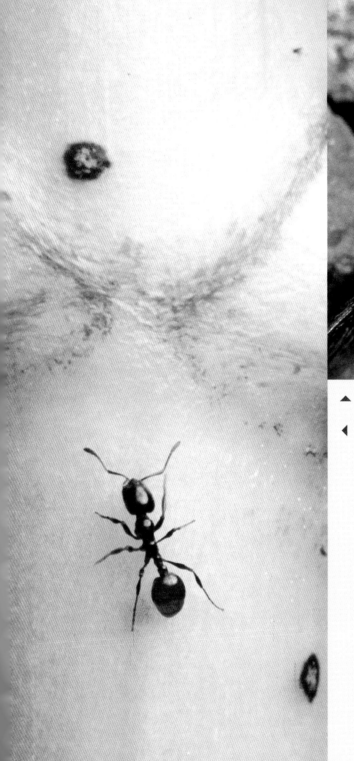

▲ **Meat Ants**

◀ **Ant on a Stem**

Some species of ants, such as fire ants, have a stinger. The stinger is not barbed, so the ants can sting more than once. Others, such as wood ants, do not have a stinger. Instead, they spray their **predators** with a poisonous fluid called formic acid.

5

▲ **Bulldog Ants at Nest Entrance**

THEIR NESTS

All ants are social and live in colonies, or nests. Most ants make their nests underground by digging out tunnels and chambers. Some, such as army ants, are **nomadic**. They do not build permanent nests. At night they rest by linking their legs together and hanging from a branch or hollow tree trunk.

The size of an ant nest varies from one species to another. Some are small and may have only a few hundred members, while others can have many thousands.

Some ants build a large pile of soil, leaves, or grass over their nest.

▼ **Mound over a Meat Ant's Nest**

7

Weaver ants build their nests using living leaves. Worker ants line up in a row along the edges of leaves. They pull the edges together using their jaws and legs. One worker holds a weaver ant **larva** in its jaws. The larva is gently squeezed to produce silk. This silk is used to glue the edges of the leaves together. The ants leave the row one at a time as the leaves are glued together.

If the nest is disturbed or threatened, the ants tap on the leaves to warn others in the nest.

Weaver Ants Building a Nest ▶

Members of an Ant Colony

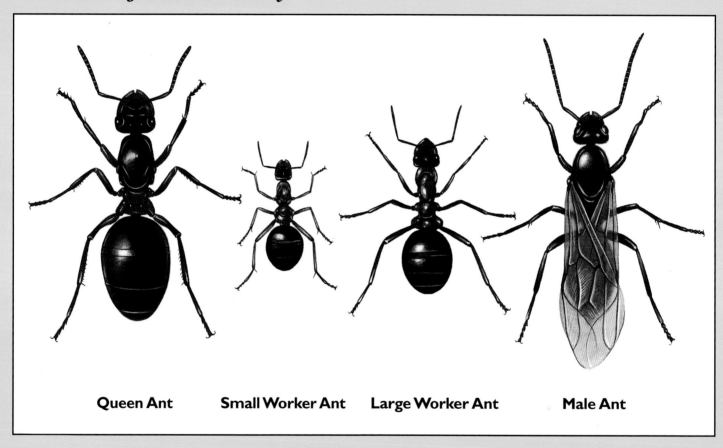

Queen Ant   Small Worker Ant   Large Worker Ant   Male Ant

THE MEMBERS OF AN ANT COLONY

Three main types of adult ants can be found in a colony.

Queen

The queen is a large, wingless female. Her only job is to lay eggs. In some species, there is more than one queen in each colony.

Workers

The workers are small, wingless females. Most ants in a colony are workers. Their job is to collect food, feed the young, defend the colony, and build the nest. They do not lay eggs. Some species have larger workers, called soldiers, which defend the colony.

Males

The males of the colony have wings. They do not work; their sole job is to **mate** with young queen ants.

HOW ANTS COLLECT FOOD

In most ant species, workers go out to search for food on their own. When a worker finds a new food source, it returns to the colony, laying a scent trail. This trail leads other workers to the food. They follow the scent, forming a column. Then they collect the food and bring it back to the nest.

Different kinds of ants have different ways of collecting and storing food. Most ants are **scavengers**. Some are hunters, some are harvesters, some are gardeners, and some are honey-dew collectors. The bulldog ant is a solitary hunter.

◄ **Bulldog Ant Eating a Dead Insect**

▲ Ants Moving in a Column

Scavengers

Most ants are scavengers; they feed on animals as well as plants. Animal foods include dead or dying insects and spiders. Plant foods include rotting fruit.

Sometimes ants enter people's houses. They scavenge food such as sugar, cheese, meat, and bread.

▼ **Ants Scavenging on a Dead Beetle**

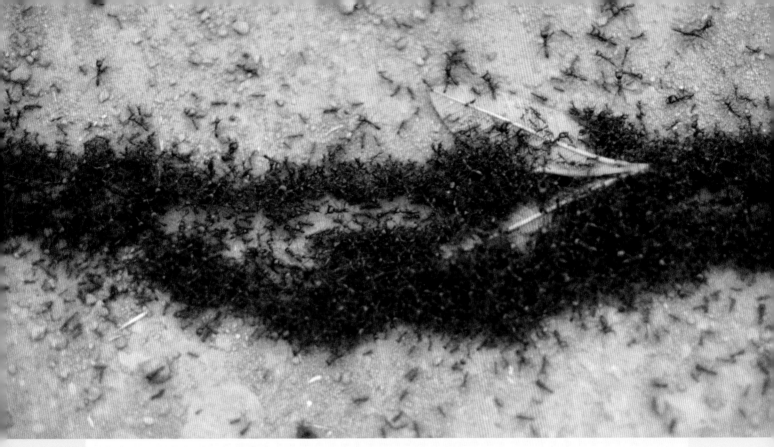

A Column of Driver Ants ▲

Hunters

Some hunter ants, such as army ants and driver ants, are fierce predators. They hunt and kill living animals. Unlike most ants, their workers do not search for food on their own. Instead, a large number of ants go out together in a **swarm**. They eat every living animal in their path. They feed mainly on insects and spiders, but their **prey** can include much larger animals.

Leafcutter Ants Collecting Pieces of Leaves ▲

Harvester Ants Collecting Seeds ▶

Harvesters

Harvester ants collect seeds and scavenge on dead insects. They store the collected seeds in underground nests. Before each seed is stored, the ants remove the seed husk, or outer covering. When food is scarce, the ants chew the seeds into a mush. This mush is called ant bread, which is used to feed the colony.

Gardeners

Worker leafcutter ants cut off pieces of leaves from plants. They carry the pieces back to their nest, holding them above their heads. Inside the nest, the leaves are chewed into a mush. This mush is used to grow a bed of fungus. The fungus is then fed to the ant larvae.

Honeydew Collectors

Many ant species are honeydew collectors—they gather and eat the honeydew produced by insects such as aphids and scale insects.

Honeypot ants are **unique**. They live in dry areas where food may become scarce. When food is plentiful, the workers collect honeydew from plants and insects. Back in the nest, they feed the honeydew to special worker ants called repletes.

Each replete stores honeydew in its stomach, which expands to many times its normal size. Because they cannot walk, the repletes hang from the ceiling of the nest chamber. When food is needed, the repletes regurgitate the honeydew to feed the other ants in the nest.

◀ **Meat Ants Collecting Honeydew from Scale Insects**

▲ **Honeypot Ants Hanging from the Roof of Their Nest**

Bulldog Ant Workers with Larvae ▲

THEIR LIFE CYCLE

At certain times of the year, ant colonies produce winged males and queens. In many species, these males and queens fly into the air, where they mate. The males die soon after mating. Some new queens leave the colony and begin their own nests.

The **life cycle** of the ant has four stages: egg, larva, pupa, and adult.

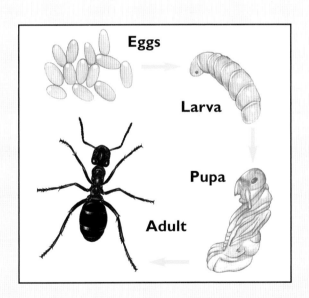

Once an adult ant hatches, it does not grow any larger.

ANTS AND THEIR IMPORTANCE TO HUMANS

How They Are Useful

- Ants are an important part of the **food chain**. They clean up dead insects and other dead animals.
- Some ant species help farmers by killing insects that damage crops.
- Ants that build underground nests turn over the soil and enrich it.

▼ **Ants Eating a Dead Rat**

Ants Eating a Sandwich ▲

How They Are Harmful

- Many types of ants can be pests when they enter houses.
- Some ants nest in the wooden parts of houses and can cause damage.
- Some ants, such as fire ants, can inflict painful stings. If an animal or a human receives a large number of these stings, they can be deadly.

GLOSSARY

antennae: Thin, movable parts of an insect's head that help it to sense its surroundings

food chain: A term used to describe how all living things, predators and prey, feed on other living things in order to survive

habitats: The places where animals and plants live and grow

larva: Immature, early-stage forms of animals

life cycle: The stages, or phases, of an animal's development

mate: To join with another animal in order to produce offspring

nomadic: Moving from place to place

predators: Animals that hunt, catch, and eat other animals

prey: Animals that are hunted and eaten by other animals

scavengers: Animals that eat rotting flesh and fruit, or food left behind by others

species: Types of animals that have some physical characteristics in common

swarm: A very large number of insects moving together

tropical: Areas that are very warm throughout the year

unique: Something that is different for each person or animal

INDEX

abdomen, 4
antennae, 4
army ants, 7, 15

bulldog ant, 12

colonies, 7, 21

driver ants, 15

fire ants, 5, 23
food chain, 22
formic acid, 5

gardeners, 12

harvester ants, 17
harvesters, 12

honeydew collectors, 12, 18
honeypot ants, 18
hunter ants, 15
hunters, 12

jaws, 4, 8

larva(e), 8, 17, 21
leafcutter ants, 17
legs, 4, 7, 8
life cycle, 21

nest(s), 7, 8, 11, 12, 17, 18, 21, 22, 23

predators, 15
prey, 15
pupa, 21

queen(s), 11, 21

repletes, 18

scavengers, 14
scent trail, 12
swarm, 15

termites, 2
thorax, 4

weaver ants, 8
"white ants," 2
wood ants, 5